Just Sisters

Just Sisters

You Mess With Her, You Mess With Me

 WILLOW CREEK PRESS

Published by Willow Creek Press
P.O. Box 147, Minocqua, Wisconsin 54548

Photo Credits: p2 © Ron Kimball/ronkimballstock.com; p6 © Lisa & Mike Husar/www.teamhusar.com; p9 © Anup Shah/naturepl.com; p10 © Frans Lanting/Minden Pictures; p13 © John Daniels/Ardea.com; p14 © Erwin & Peggy Bauer/Bruce Coleman, Inc.; p17 © Lisa & Mike Husar/www.teamhusar.com; p18 © Shin Yoshino/Minden Pictures; p21 © Tui De Roy/Minden Pictures; p22 © Jane Burton/Bruce Coleman, Inc.; p25 © Wild Images/ronkimballstock.com; p26 © Tom & Pat Lesson/Ardea.com; p29 © Lisa & Mike Husar/www.teamhusar.com; p30 © Daniel J. Cox/naturalexposures.com; p33 © Frederic Rolland/Ardea.com; p34 © ZSSD/Minden Pictures; p37,38 © Anup Shah/naturepl.com; p41 © Lisa & Mike Husar/www.teamhusar.com; p42 © Michio Hoshino/Minden Pictures; p44,47 © Daniel J. Cox/naturalexposures.com; p48 © Frederic Rolland/Ardea.com; p51 © Hayden Oake/Ardea.com; p52 © Ron Kimball/ronkimballstock.com; p55 © www.artwolfe.com; p56 © M. Watson/Ardea.com; p59 © Ron Kimball/ronkimballstock.com; p60 © Martin Harvey/Peter Arnold, Inc.; p63 © Sumio Harada/Minden Pictures; p64 © Konrad Wothe/Minden Pictures; p67 © Klein/Peter Arnold, Inc.; p68 © John Daniels/Ardea.com; p71 © Jean Michel Labat/Ardea.com; p72,75© Daniel J. Cox/naturalexposures.com; p76 © Mitsuaki Iwago/Minden Pictures; p78 © Javier Flores/ronkimballstock.com; p81 © Lisa & Mike Husar/www.teamhusar.com; p82 © Matthias Breiter/Minden Pictures; p85 © David Madison/Bruce Coleman, Inc.; p86 © Jean Michel Labat/Ardea.com; p89 © Peter Blackwell/naturepl.com; p90 © Ron Kimball/ronkimballstock.com; p93 © Mitsuaki Iwago/Minden Pictures; p94 © John Daniels/Ardea.com;

Design: Donnie Rubo
Printed in China

Dedication
For Laura and Vanessa

Acknowledgements
Thanks to Ginger and Sugar whose tugging, stalking, chasing
and snuggling are a fountain of sisterly inspiration.

Thanks to Jill,
the best big sister a kid could ever want.

Thanks to Joyce and Carole, my step-sisters, for teaching me about
the joy and pain of sisterhood. Carole, you will forever be missed.

Thanks to my editor, Andrea Donner,
for her superb ability to tweak.

Intimacy&
Inspiration

I, who have no sisters or brothers,

look with some degree

of innocent envy on those who may be

said to be born to friends . . .

———

James Boswell (1740-1795)
Scottish-born author

We had exactly one sister apiece. We grew up knowing the simple arithmetic of scarcity: A sister is more precious than an eye.

———

Barbara Kingsolver
Sisters Dayspring Calendar

With a sister you never have

to censor your words.

We talk about everything and nothing.

———

Sheryl Glass
sister of Nancy Glass, television host, writer and producer

A sister's heart is the safest place
to bury all your secrets.

———

B. Kuchler

I can tell you my fears,

which are made lighter by being shared.

———

Pamela Winterbourne
American writer

We know one another's faults,

virtues, catastrophes, mortifications, triumphs,

rivalries, desires, and how long we can each

hang by our hands to a bar.

———

Dame Emilie Rose Macaulay (1881-1958)
English novelist

It's very hard in this world to find

someone who can walk in your shoes,

but you come closer to that than anybody.

———

Coretta Scott King (1927-2006)
in a letter to her sister Edythe

Sisters examine each other so they
can have a map for how they should behave.

———

Michael D. Kahn
American psychologist and educator

My sister and I,

without knowing it at the time,

were teaching each other

how to find solutions to tough situations.

———

Phoebe Elizabeth Sisk
American writer

It's hard to be responsible, adult,

and sensible all the time.

How good it is to have a sister

whose heart is as young as your own.

———

Pam Brown
American author

Roots & Memories

Our brothers and sisters are there with us
from the dawn of our personal stories
to the inevitable dusk.

———

Susan Scarf Merrell
American author

I find that as I grow older,

I love those most whom I loved first.

———

Thomas Jefferson (1743-1826)
Third President of the United States

The bond that joined us lay
deeper than outward things;
The rivers of our souls spring
from the same well!

———

Po Chu-I (772–846)
Chinese poet

To be rooted is perhaps the most important
and least recognized need of the human soul.

———

Simone Weil (1909-1943)
French Philosopher

So many shared memories rest between sisters.

Some, like a sleeping grizzly bear,

seem best left undisturbed.

While others can fill a rainy afternoon

with laughter and sunshine.

———

Melody Carlson
American author

Y ou and I are tied together
by years of misunderstandings,
cross words, icy silences, laughter,
hugs, tenderness, and love.
All those strands are twisted into a knot
that nothing will ever, ever break.

———

Ellyn Sanna
American author

Today is far from Childhood—

But up and down the hills

I held her hand the tighter—

Which shortened all the miles—

———

Emily Dickinson (1830-1886)
American poet

My sister and me,

treasurers of each other's childhoods,

linked by volatile love,

best friends who make other best friends

ever so slightly less best.

———

Patricia Volk
American author

To the outside world we all grow old.

But not to brothers and sisters.

We know each other as we always were . . .

We live outside the touch of time.

———

Clara Ortega
American writer

Comfort & Camaraderie

Y ou mess with her,

you mess with me.

———

Maria Smedstad
American author

Sisters are...

a port in each other's storms.

———

Elizabeth Fishel
American author

Help one another,

is part of the religion of our sisterhood.

———

Louisa May Alcott (1832-1888)
American author

Sisters...

help each other stay in good relationships,

get out of messed up ones,

pick up and start over again.

———

Linda H. Hollies
American author

The only time you look down on me is
when you're picking me up from the floor.

———

Maria Smedstad
American author

A sister is sometimes the only person who sees the horizon from your point of view.

Mia Evans
American writer

A sister is one who will pick you up
when you are down.
If she cannot pick you up
she will lie down beside you and listen.

———

Unknown

Is solace anywhere more comforting

than in the arms of sisters?

———

Alice Walker
American writer

Appreciation & Aggravation

If you don't understand how a woman
could both love her sister dearly and want
to wring her neck at the same time,
then you were probably an only child.

———

Linda Sunshine
American author

One day you are wanting

to rearrange her personality ever so slightly.

...but the bottom line is this:

you will always love her, no matter what.

Unconditionally.

———

Whitney Otto
American author

Sibling relationships... outlast marriages,
survive the death of parents,
resurface after quarrels that would
sink any friendship.

———

Erica E. Goode
American writer

However frank you might think
you're being with friends,
honesty reaches a different level
between sisters.

———

Sandra Deeble
American author

She is your partner in crime,

your midnight companion...

She is your teacher, your defense attorney,

your personal press agent, even your shrink.

Some days, she's the reason you wish

you were an only child.

———

Barbara Alpert
American author

Features alone do not run in the blood;
vices and virtues, genius and folly,
are transmitted through the same sure
but unseen channel.

———

William Hazlitt
English author

If your sister is in a tearing hurry to go
out and cannot catch your eye,
she's wearing your best sweater.

Pam Brown
American author

Sisters define their rivalry in terms of competition for the gold cup of parental love. It is never perceived as a cup which runneth over, rather a finite vessel from which the more one sister drinks, the less is left for the others.

————

Elizabeth Fishel
American author

One of the best things about being an
adult is the realization that you can
share with your sister and
still have plenty for yourself.

———

Betsy Cohen
American writer

Similarity&
Individuality

Sister relationships are a study in contrasts—
we may be polar opposites of each other,
or different shades on the
same color spectrum.

———

Ellyn Sanna
American author

W e were threads of the same cloth...
when blended together it turned into
the most beautiful of fabrics.

———

Diane Burke
American poet

Of two sisters

one is always the watcher,

one the dancer.

———

Louise Glück
American author and poet

Sisters are like different instruments
in a band, or different voices in a chorus,
because you are not exactly alike,
you harmonize in beautiful ways.

———

Margaret Lannamann
American author

If Sadie is molasses, then I am vinegar.

She is sugar and I'm the spice.

———

Bessie Delany (about her 103-year-old sister, Sadie)
American author

A sister is like a mirror in which you can

see a part of yourself reflected.

———

Joan Walsh Anglund
American author

Two different faces,

but in tight places

we think and we act as one.

———

Our siblings resemble us just enough
to make all their differences confusing,

———

Susan Scarf Merrell
American author

We will always be sisters.
Our differences may never go away,
but neither, for me, will our song.

———

Nancy Kelton
American writer